I0847129

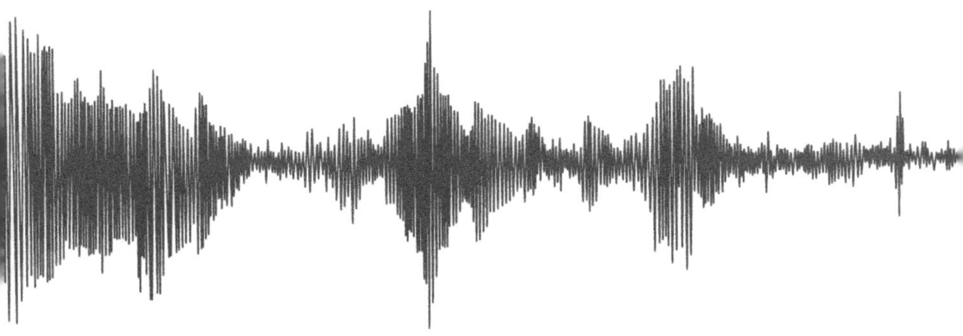

fine tuning

Kerry Love

Empress Mode, LLC
ISBN: 979-8-9889945-7-2

Book design by Kerry Love

                    "A Poem"

A poem can rhyme,
A poem can chime,
A poem is sad,
A poem is glad,
A poem can be funny,
A poem can be sunny,
A poem is neat,
A poem's a treat,
A poem can make you laugh,
A poem can make you cry,
A poem is very special,
And I wrote this poem to tell you why.

By Kerry Spengler
Grade 4
Sterling Park Elementary
Teacher: Joan Daley

ACKNOWLEDGMENTS

Special thanks to Jill, my best everything, for helping me fine-tune most of this life and 1000 past ones – at least since forever. And to Alicia, my sister who understands me like no other. I am so grateful for you and our strange little family.

Thank you to Ali Ferguson for your love, magic, and editorial skills.

To the dear ones who gave me such great feedback on this book, especially Desi Draws, Hugo Hanriot, Becky Rostkowski, and my mom.

And to all of my friends and family over the globe, your love and support have meant the world to me. A thousand thank yous and many lifetimes of love. Always.

FINE TUNING

The dial spins
The compass turns
You walk away
And my heart yearns
I'm sad and fine
I laugh and mourn
It's time again
To be reborn
I stretch and cry
I move and shake
I analyze
Each damn mistake
I find myself
I love her more
I learn a thing
I do a chore
And then it's time
To make some art
Creating gold
From broken heart
The stars will shift
The flowers bloom
I love it all
When I fine tune

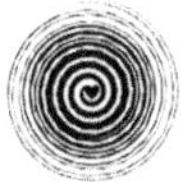

CONTENTS

CONTENTS

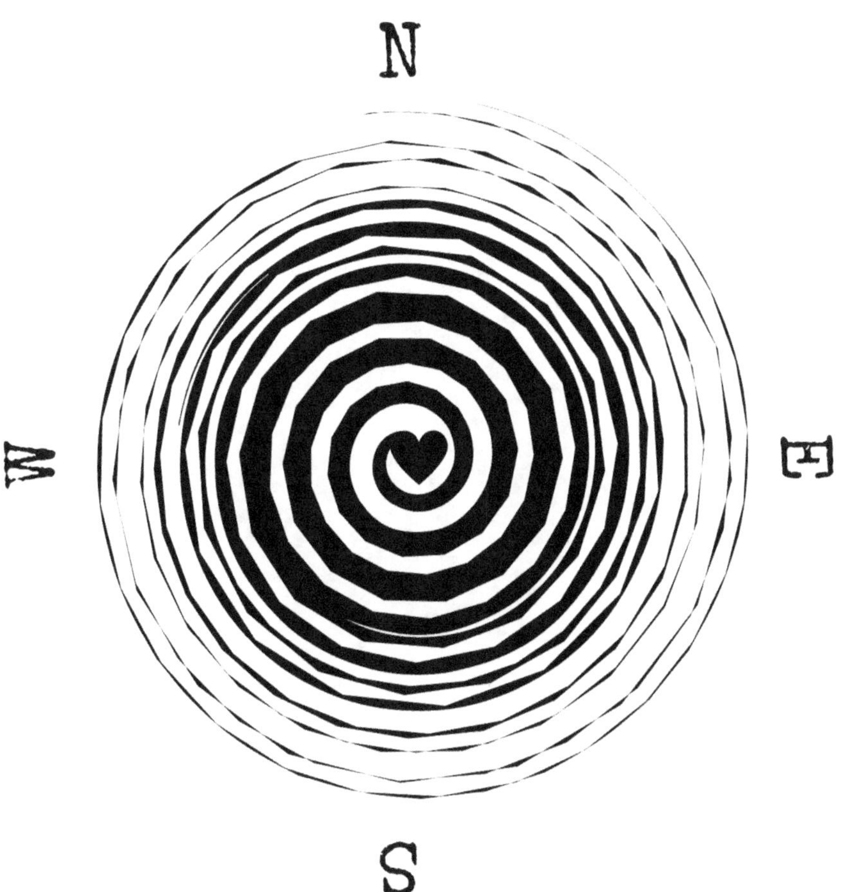

N
W
E
S

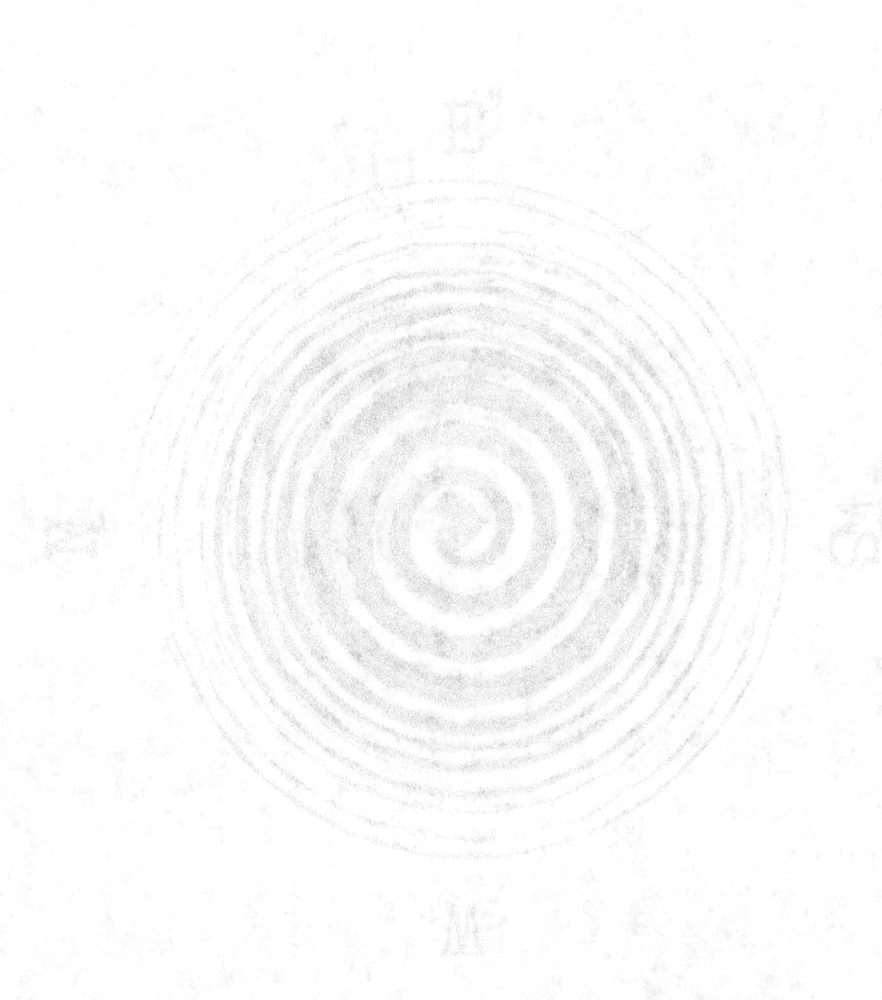

EAST

Make time
Make it just for you
Make it last
Pay attention
Notice the moments
You feel more like you
Go make more of them
Make time
Go feel alive
For god's sake
Feel alive

TRUTH

Truth
Solid as sunbeams
Rises in understanding at dawn
Shining with hope
To meet the midday
Blazing with confidence
And blinding obstinance
It charges through the afternoon
Burning everything in its path
Then finally in the evening
Falling toward the earth
In a slow and brilliant spectacle
Until we are left
In the dark
Alone together

IT'S TIME

You are a rose
Set to bloom
When the sun and the moon
Have determined
It's time
When you have been
Both nurtured and nourished
Do not let
Clumsy, desperate hands
Peel open your petals
Before it's time
Reveal yourself slowly
Unfurling your majesty
Sharing your sweet scent
As you continue
To reach for the light

BE BRAVE

I want to be brave
I want to be the kind of person
Who speaks her truth
Unabashedly
And (like someone who is not me once said)
Even if my voice shakes
That kind of person is free
I want to believe the people who tell me
That sharing my words helps them
But that is a level of belief
I haven't quite found in myself
And so their words wash over me
In a gentle wave that never quite makes it
To the shore of my heart
I want to be the woman
I came here to be
One that believes in the importance of her own words
-Not just the poetry
But in the words she dishes out
To her friends and her students
In great, heaping scoops
Be brave. Be brave. Be brave.
(A heartbeat)
I want to trust in the magic that comes through me
And not turn down my light
Just because it has scared so many
In the shadows

I want to have the courage
To wait for the man
Who craves the full force of my sunlight
Because he knows
That's what makes trees stronger
And I want to have the courage
To let him go
When his leaves no longer
Turn toward me
I want to have the strength
To be my own tree
And my own sun
To grow and shine
And remember
That being fearless
Is being free
And being free is
Everything

STEP ONE

Just love your life
Even when it's hard
It's still yours
It's only yours
Just keep making choices
That help you
Love it a little more
One step
At a time

A CERTAINTY OF PURPOSE

I am watching a tiny bug
So small I can barely see him
And yellow in the least cheery sense
Not the bold lemon
But the yellow of old paper
And decaying wedding gowns
He is walking across my sketchpad
And suddenly I am looking at the paper differently
The texture so uneven
Pulpy up close
But convincingly smooth from any other distance
I draw a line with my pencil
He crosses it without hesitation
I draw a line with my pen
He crosses that too
It is the same
With the circle that I draw around him
So I bear down on the paper
Making both a line and a groove
He just keeps going
With what seems like
A certainty of purpose
I wonder how many little bugs like this
I have crushed accidentally
Never knowing they were there
I wonder what is his purpose
Does he even know?
Or is he just walking forward
Until he can walk forward no more
Then I wonder
Am I?

FISSION

I went back
To the beginning
Of us
To the soul-searing
Pain
Of our birth
From each other
Like fire
It was beautiful
And it burned

B
E
S
A

A WAY

Meet me in a dream
Where I am a star
And you are a black hole
Pulling me closer
While it tears me apart
Meet me in a dream
Where I am sand
And you are the ocean
Crashing into me
And dragging tiny pieces away
Meet me in a dream
Where you are the pine
And I am the cypress
Sapplings intertwined
Growing together
Seeking the same light
Meet me in a dream
And let me show you
My love
In a way
These words
Cannot

TOGETHER

I love that we are trying this thing
Together
This cracking open
To show each other
The truth inside
This slicing off and tentatively holding out
Pieces of ourselves
To be sampled
This gently pressing
Parts of us together
To see if they fit
I don't know
If we will decide
Each day
To continue this dance
Together
Even if you would promise me that
(We both have been there before)
You cannot
And so I stay here
In the breaking and sharing
The whispering uncertainty
The boundless possibility
And I try to remember
To breathe and be grateful
For you and me
And the miracle it is
That we are trying this thing
Together

ANIMAL

Sometimes
I am surprised
By the animal
I become
When I
Think of you

HER

He doesn't understand
How someone so particular
About everything
Her pens
Her tea
The three kinds of butter
(One for baking
One for cooking
One for eating on piece after piece of toast)
Which blanket is for
Cuddling on the couch
And which is for
Snuggling in bed
And why there is a difference
He doesn't understand
How someone so particular
About everything
Can love
Everyone
He doesn't understand
Her

WOUNDED

He called me girl
And it made me cringe
I had worked far too long
And hard
At becoming
A woman
To ever be called a girl again
By him
Or anyone
If I thought about it
I had never actually been a girl
Not even as a child
I had really
Only ever been
A wounded animal

ON PURPOSE

I don't know
What is harder
About being a human
That we sometimes
Accidentally kill
Other living things
Or that we sometimes
Do it on purpose

WHY ARE YOU CRYING

Why are you crying
They asked me
I guess it's because
We don't protect children
And the people most hellbent
On saying they are protecting children
Are doing the most damage
Or maybe I'm crying because
I am still the child who wasn't protected
And it's taken me forty years to reclaim
My Body
Only for my country to tell me
That it's not really my body at all
And that makes me really angry
And really sad
So maybe I'm crying because
I am so fucking strong
That I don't let fear keep me
From my emotions
Anymore
I feel deeply
So I can heal deeply
Because that is the
Only
Path to love
And I will settle for
Nothing less

Because if we're not here
For love
Why are we even here?
And so I have to cry
And I have to heal
Because when we heal
Everything heals
When we change
Everything changes
So why am I crying
Why aren't you?

BREADCRUMBS

I will not say
Come back
I cannot
Beg for you
I want only
What wants me
But I can
Break this bread
Drop these crumbs
Hoping
That you will
Find your way

YOUR SHIRT

I have decided to keep it
The love you gave me
And the shirt you left behind
I almost threw it out
After you called and said
You were taking space
(For you is what you said
From me is what you meant)
I almost set it free
Right into the trash
The love, the shirt
You
But today
I went down to the basement
And saved it, your shirt
And put it on
It felt good
Really good
Like the love you gave me
So I decided
To keep them both

EPILOGUE
I have discarded your shirt
I wasn't going to
Thought maybe you would
Come back for it (or me)
But I chose to let it go
When you chose to let me go
I cut it up
Like your words cut me up
So there would be no coming back
Which shouldn't bother you
If what you said was true
I was never going to choose you

FROZEN

The roses in the vase
Have lasted longer
Than anyone
Would have guessed
They seem frozen
In time
Half-dead
But not yet wilted
Stuck somewhere between
Like my heart
When I think
Of you

LESS

I have been told
That I am difficult
Dangerous even
From people who claimed to love me
(But were capable only
Of trying to control me)
I was told to dilute myself
Dumb myself down
Or I would be
Alone
Maybe forever
But as I fall in love
With the fullness of who I am
These words are absurd
Make myself less?
Why?
(So you don't need to be more?)
Or what?
I will never get a man?
A man?!
You must mean a half-human
Who else would be happy
With only tiny bits of me
Certainly not a man
But maybe someone who has been coddled
By a world that gave their words more value
And deemed their jokes more funny
And how many women
Have faked laughter

And interest
And orgasms
To be with these half-humans
Fragile beings who take more
Than they could ever give?
Because maybe something
Is better than nothing?
No thank you
If I must change who I am
To win the fleeting affection of someone
Half as interesting
Half as smart
Half as loving
As me?
No thank you
Their fear tells me I will be alone
My heart tells me that is just fine
If my life alone offers me more of myself
Than my life with you
(Being smaller so you feel safe)
You are the one who is alone
You are the one who must change
Go then with your pride
And your vanity
And your snowglobe ego
Go and find your spine
And your heart
Become a man
And never speak to me of changing again
If alone
I am everything
Without me
You are nothing

POISON

Indignation
Is the cheapest high
Most addictive when righteous
It will demand a fix
Until you
Recount
Retell
Revisit
Becoming so enamored with
This poison
You believe it to be a
Truth worth
The sacrifice of your soul

OUTSIDE

Somehow
I let the outside
Make me forget
Who I have always been
On the inside
Free

———

Somehow
I needed the outside
To help me remember
Who I have always been
On the inside
Free

PAPER

I am
A piece of paper
Torn
Making a sound
Both whispery
And sharp
I'm two dimensional now
Stripped of my body
I am paper
But paper cuts
And burns
And holds the words
That change the world
I am paper

FARTHER AWAY

I always cry on airplanes
Whether I am coming or going
Doesn't seem to matter
Maybe it's because I can feel
The hellos and goodbyes
Of the loves reunited
And those gone forever
The whispers of
I've missed you
It's been so long
I can't believe you're gone
Echos of the past
Foretelling the future
All in the same cramped seat
Where I sit
Maybe that's why I cry
Or maybe it's for
My own broken heart
And my gratitude
For being nearer my creator
But farther away

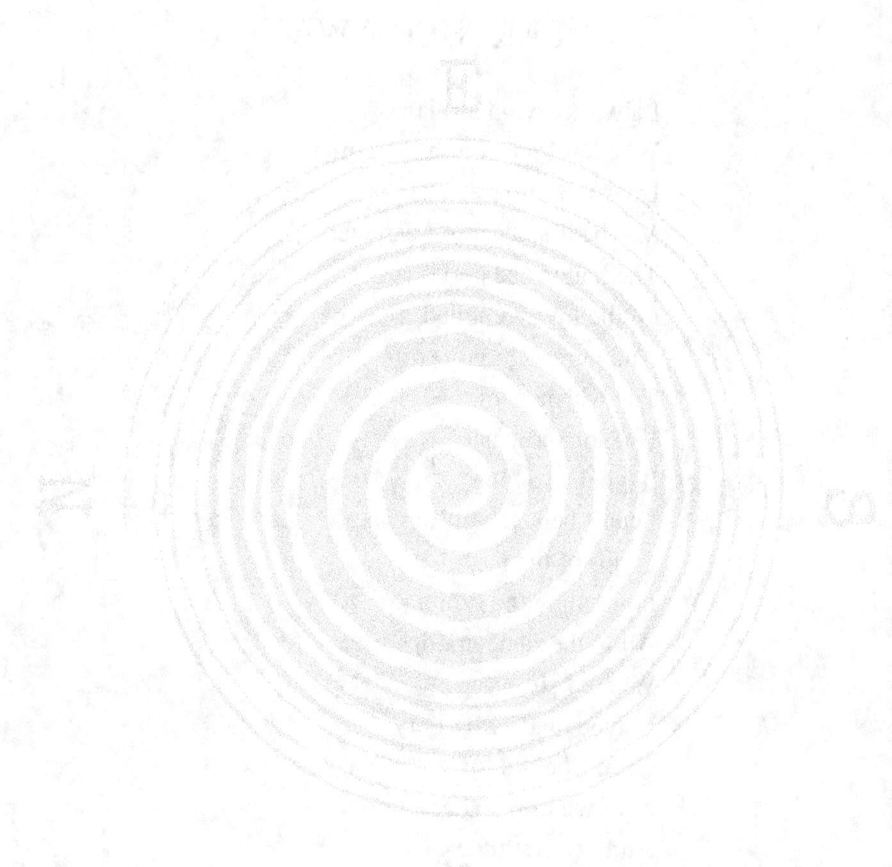

FOSSIL

There is poetry inside me
Written just for you
But you will never read it
Though it's real and sharp and true
I cannot freeze in time
The galaxy of us
I will not trap in amber
The peace shared in our touch
To remember it was real
Would simply hurt too much

NO CHOICE

It doesn't cost me
Nothing
To love this hard
Sometimes I think I will
Lose myself
And never come back
Sometimes I think
There must be an easier way
But then I remember
Who I am
And there is
No choice

SPARKLERS

I avoid fear
Like I am at the grocery store
In my hometown
Wearing sweatpants
And I have just seen someone
I went to high school with
(Or worse, an old crush)
So I am ducking down aisles
Hoping to get away before we have to
Intentionally avoid eye contact
Pretending we don't
See one another, know one another
Or worse, the awkward chit and chat
About so and so
While pretending we are not sizing each other up
Pretending is a state I avoid
Like fear
Because I forget that my fear
Is not some acquaintance in a grocery store
It is not a lukewarm coffee-breath-of-an-experience
(Mildly unpleasant and therefore unforgivable)

No, my fear is intimate
A bath of needle-sharp heat
Pop rocks on my skin
Like my whole body is a tongue
Eager to be fed
Eager to be loved
So I gather my fear, instead of backing away
(It's not easy)
It feels like I am wrapping my arms
Around a bunch of lit sparklers
Tiny bright pieces of fire
And I love it
I love my fear
Until those little burns
Feel good

BEING BURNED

Here is a secret
We hold onto our pain
Some of us
Hold it so close
We need it for the warmth
Not sure who we are
Without it
Because being burned
Feels better
Than being
Nothing at all

BAGGAGE

The fairy tale
Is real
Happily ever after
Exists
Come join me
But I must warn you
You will need to unload
Some baggage
If you want
To fly

SOUTH

Make space
Make it just for you
Make space
In your heart
And in your life
Release what doesn't work
Or isn't yours
So there is room for something new
Something you
Make space
Go feel alive
For god's sake
Feel alive

LEAD

Beliefs are not statues
Permanent fixtures
To cling to
Or hide behind
The are living, breathing partners
We dance with
Coming together, moving apart
As the music changes
Will they lead or
Will you?

SAVING

When I was drowning
I did not look
At what was on the other end
Of the life rope
I just grabbed hold
And survived
I did what I did
To become the version of me
That no longer needs
Saving
And no longer punishes myself
For the choices I made
When I was drowning

THE DEVIL

I had dinner with the devil
Once
It was a really nice date
He held the door
And ordered for us
And watched me intently
With his ice blue eyes
At the end of the night
After he paid the check
He kissed me
While he wrapped
His thick fingers
Around my throat
And squeezed
I think it broke him
When he saw no fear
I had dinner with the devil
Once
And that was enough

THE THINGS

Sometimes I wonder
If am more sorry
About the things I got wrong
Or the things
I didn't

OKAY

What am I forgetting?
Is my mantra lately
(Because there is always something)
To run the vacccuuummm
How to spell vacccuuuummm
My worth
What am I forgetting
Someone's birthday
To text you back
My keys
What am I forgetting
To be present
Not to judge
To drink more water
That I am made of light
To love more
To fear less
To breathe
What am I forgetting
That even when it's not
Everything is okay

FLUENT

It seems that I am fluent
In the language "I don't know"
Though not my mother tongue
I have come to love it so
There's many things that I don't know
Perhaps you can relate
What to do and where to go
The time, the month, the date
I used to know most everything
I'd tell you and it's true
But I don't know a thing at all
Since I fell in love with you

WHERE THEY BELONG

I want to live
Inside your chest
Like a little bird
(Some people's hearts are cages
But the door was blown off yours
So I will always feel free)
I want your bones
To be my walls
And the air I breathe
To smell like you
So even in the springtime
When the lilacs are blooming
Your scent and theirs
Are unmistakably intertwined
Like you and me
I want your heartbeat
To set the rhythm of my life
The cadence to my melody
A soundtrack to which we dance
I want us to melt into one another
Not through inertia
Or desperation
But by choice
And by no other choice
The way geese fly south in the winter
And ducks nest near the stream
For nourishment
And because
It's where they belong

AGAIN

I knew
When we found
The dead white moth
That it was time
To let you
Go
With faith
That anything
Seeking light
Will be
Resurrected

OSIRIS

He was born upon a Sunday
The only man I've ever met
He had a giant crater
In the middle of his chest
I knew I couldn't fill it
He would never quite be whole
But I hoped he'd let me linger there
To just be with his soul
Then one day he'd invite me in
And give me space to start
To carve off pieces of my own
And build him a new heart
It wouldn't beat the same
As the one he'd had before
But pieces of a shattered heart
Can sometimes love you more

STATIC

When the static is heavy
And our paths are apart
Remember you know me
I am here in your heart
When your mind starts spinning
And asks what I meant
And makes up some story
About the time that we spent
Go home to your heart
Where I'll always be
Waiting for you
To come back to me

BREAK

I want to smell my hair again
And breathe the scent of you
To know it wasn't just pretend
Those things we chose to do

I want to watch your head again
Between my breasts and thighs
And see you look up at me
With those sad, sad bedroom eyes

I want to feel your touch again
And the soft waves of your hair
I want to hear you cough again
When you act like you don't care

I want to kiss your lips again
Your forehead and your palms
I break a little every day
I can't be in your arms

But if I smelled my hair again
And if it smelled like you
The waiting would be worth the break
And all that we've been through

Because love like this
It only comes once upon a time
I just don't want to miss a life
When I can call you mine

YET

The ache is sweet
This present fear of letting you go
Like jasmine heavy
In the Carolina heat
So pungently sweet
It stings your eyes, your nose
Almost burns your throat
Yet
If distilled and
Perfectly blended with
Just the right other note
This ache could
Make a perfume so timeless
Like a madeleine
And a universe

HOLY

You can keep your church
With your book of rules
Stolen from other mouths
Ripped from their source
And cobbled back together
As chains
While you sit in your pew
Of exclusion
Under your cross
Of oppression
And make your checks out to
An agenda
I will walk the woods
Baptized by rain
Listening to the stream preach
And the choir of birds
I will take dew drops of communion
On my tongue
While I genuflect
Before the trees and ancient rocks
Letting their peace fill my heart
I will feel the earth, the sun, the breeze
And praise the sky, the flowers, and bees
Now you tell me
Which one of us
Is worshipping
God

NEVERMORE

When your raven
Came to call
And asked me
Do I still at all
Love you as
I did before
I said I've never
Loved you more

WATCHING

I am not sorry
That I don't have time to follow the news
And to make small talk with you
About the economy or the weather
Or any other made up thing
I am not sorry
That I don't want to make more money
To hustle or to grind
Or any other made up thing
But my dog, you see,
He's more than a dog
And some day
I'm going to have to live without him
So I have to spend my time
Watching him
And trying to remember

DOC

There is a prayer I say
When I walk behind him
And watch him sniff the world
Tail wagging
Especially after a snow melt
When there are
So
Many
Smells
Or when I watch him sleep
Curled up like a kitten
Or spread out
With his paws twitching
There is a prayer I say
When I kiss his face
That smells like corn flakes
Or when he greets me
Grinning and whining
Full of joy at being reunited
Even after the briefest separation
There is a prayer I say
When he farts
And it smells so bad
It forces me out of what I'm doing
And into a laugh
Despite my burning eyes

Or when his mouth is dry and
His curled lip
Sticks to his tooth
Like he is giving me
His best impression of Elvis
There is a prayer I say
Whenever I remember
Thank you god
Thank you god
Thank you god

SHARP

There are moments where
I'm sure
That I don't
Exist
Like I am slipped into
The pocket
Of someone else's time
A forgotten dime
Only a footnote
Never a book of my own
How can I feel
Everything
And nothing
And how can they both
Be so sharp?

MY SHORE

It has been so long
Since I've heard your voice
I think maybe you don't exist
Sometimes I listen to the silence
For your voice
The way you might lift a shell
To your ear
And listen for the faint whisper of the ocean
Time has had her way with us
Like the tide
Has its way with the beach
And I wonder if
Like the tide
Time will someday bring you
Back to my shore

AT ALL

I'm sorry
I say to my friends
About still loving you
I'm sorry
I just don't know how
To stop
I say
To the ears
And hearts
That sat and witnessed and held me
As I got over you
Twice
And never really
At all
I'm sorry I say
To the ones I dare
Tell at all
The ones who
With their patient love say
It's okay, dear
We know how to
Do this
We have all
Done this before

POTENT

If you feel
Like you are being stripped
Bare
Down to your bones
Like life is taking out of you
So much
Maybe you are just being
Distilled
Maybe the world no longer needs
Who you thought you were
What you imagined you should be
Maybe nothing is being taken
Only purified
The essence
More potent

HAIKU

Knock not on my door
Until you are ready to
Face the change you seek

They say that lovers
Are mirrors to each other
I like what I see

My love, it is free
And so I give it freely
My body is not

You were not prepared
For the galaxy we made
Go then, leave me be

You asked what we were
So I asked you how you felt
Remember that peace

I am not awake
But I'm also not asleep
I am only here

SPOON

Don't stir the pot
They told me
They told us
And I tried
I really tried
To be "good"
I went to war with myself
To remain palatable
Don't stir the pot
They said
But isn't that what
Keeps things from burning?
Don't things need
To move and shift
And bump into each other a little bit?
Shouldn't everything
Have a chance
To rise to the top?
Isn't that how
We get the best
Flavor?
Don't stir the pot
They told me
And I know
That I have always been
A spoon

LIFEBOATS

I don't talk to my students
About the news of the world
Not in silent complicity
But because
I do not know what to say
About what we did
In the 80s and 90s
While we should have
Been fixing
The things that had
Been brought to our attention
Years before

I don't know how to tell them
That we got distracted
By the Rubik's cube
And Atari
And MTV
That even though we had
Sesame Street and Mr. Rogers
We still picked on
Each other
And forgot how to love

I don't know why fighting Russians
Was so vital
But I think I heard somewhere
It was about oil all along

So I'm not sure how to explain
That we were too distracted
By Dallas and Pacman
Max Headroom and New Coke
And the Space Shuttle exploding
To realize we should stop voting
For people who made laws
That didn't benefit the ones
They were supposed to represent
So I don't talk to my kids
About the news
Because I am ashamed
That we haven't done more
To protect them from ourselves

Instead, I talk to them about
Love
While I quietly try to stitch back together
These babies
Torn apart by this world
We have created for them
<Or at least didn't fight hard enough to dismantle>
I try to show them
How each piece of them holds more gold
Than they will ever need
Which is good
If it's true
And I hope it is
So I try to teach them
That there is more magic
To be found in each other
Than on the computers
In their hands

Maybe we are on the Titanic
And none of it will matter anyway
But I keep putting them
On lifeboats
Pointing them
Toward a shore
That I hope is not too littered
With jelly shoes and Happy Meal toys

Because if we are on the Titanic
I'm gonna hang out
With the band
And play my heart out
While I still
Have one

(But maybe I need to tell them
This
All of this
To ask them
Okay, beg them
Not to scroll through
Or binge watch away
Their chance to
Do right by one another
Themselves
And the world)

BURNT

I am being
Burnt inside
Like a stick of incense
Wisps of smoke
Releasing fear
And memories
Of you

44

I think it's time
To give it all away
Even the memories
Just let them all go
With the words
I think it is time
To see what flies
And what falls
And if it should all
Crash
Flaming to the ground
Well before the last wisp
Of smoke rises
To the heavens
I will be
Rebuilding

A MOMENT

When the butterfly first emerges
Wings crinkled from the cocoon
Or the phoenix shakes off
The last of the ash
I think there must be a moment
(Or a hundred)
Where they pause
And look around
And wonder
What just happened
Who am I?
What do I do now?
And maybe it takes them a moment
(Or a hundred)
To remember that they are
Everything
And they always have been
Only then, I think
Do they spread their wings
And fly

WORSHIP

It is not our fault
We were taught
To worship
The wrong things
Money
Power
Screens
Instead of
Each other
Come my love
Let me worship you

WEST

Make something

Make anything

Make it just for you

Honor yourself

Make something else

Love yourself

And maybe share it

Once you don't care what "they" think

Or get really brave

And share it when you still do

Make something

Go feel alive

For god's sake

Feel alive

STORIES

With each petal

Unfurled

The flower
Releases

Another
Story

That
Kept
Her

Trapped

In the
Bud

PONDER

I have lost
Far too much
By trying to remain
A mystery
I want to be known
And to know—
This world holds
Enough mystery
Why we're here
The depths of our own souls
So show me what you know
Of yourself
And this place
Then we can ponder the rest
Together

N
E
S
W

FAMILIAR

I loved him
From the moment I saw him
But back then I didn't know
Love
Not like I know her now
Back then I thought
A roller coaster
Was a good time
Because back then
I still mistook
Familiar
For good

JOURNEY

I c r o s s e d t h e c o u n t r y

And the place

Between who I was

And who I have

Become

On this journey

I have left

So much of myself

Behind

But what

I am coming back

To is

My heart

GREAT AND BLUE

I startled
A blue heron today
I was wandering
Off the trail
To get away from the ice
And also to imagine
That there were not
Giant houses nearby
All looking full
Of the same emptiness
I'm usually more careful
Stepping with love and
A silent prayer upon approach
That all creatures know my heart
But today my feet were heavy with joy
Oblivious
And the great great blue heron
Tucking his head under his wing
Is startled
And I am startled too
By his flight—
For a moment
We are all there is
As his great great wings
Stir the air around us

So much more than my tiny voice
Calling after him
I'm sorry
I'm sorry
I wish I had
More time with him
So I could know him better
He was great
And he was blue
Just like me
Just like you

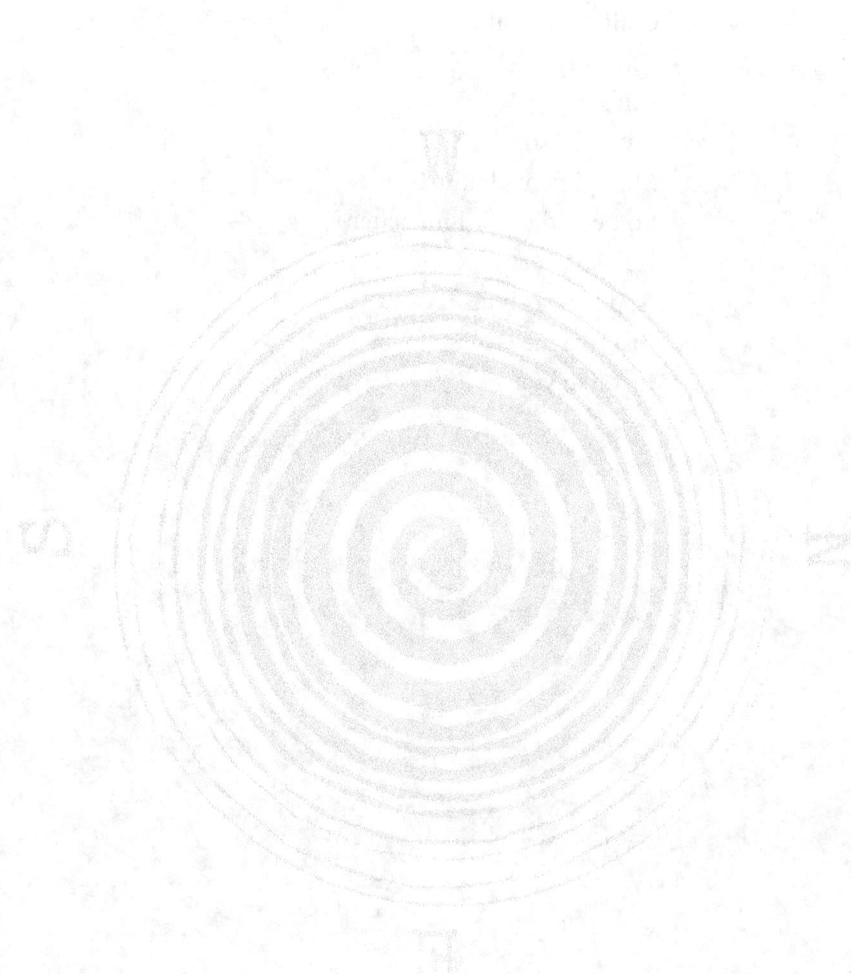

A TIME

There is a time
In Colorado
After the snows
But before the summer sun
Turns everything brown
That the giant yellow
Butterflies
Come to visit me
Singing with their wings
Little portals
Marrying time
Into a thing concrete
And elusive

FLOAT

Do you know what to do
If you get lost
He asked me
While we were hiking
Through a forest of half-devastated trees
Just find the water
And follow it he said
As I splashed my feet
And he baptized himself
In the cold, mountain creek
There is always something
Further downstream he said
And that may be true
In his mountains
But where I come from
It's flat
And watery
So when you are lost
Where I come from
All you can do
Is lie back
And float

SUMMER

There are fireworks going off outside
And my butt cheeks are itchy
From getting too much sun
On places usually well-hidden
My hair is wild and crunchy
My skin every color
Depending upon which layer
You peel back
Even blue from where I fell out of a pool
When I was trying not to feel
Self-conscious
And also blue from where I hit
My own leg with my own car door
On the first (only) date
With a warrior who cowered
When he heard my story
It is summer and I am alive
The phone pings with more matches
More men throwing their hats
Into my ring
But it would take a blow torch
To get my attention these days
Something rare and powerful
To take me away from my old dog
And this notebookBirds of all kinds
From eagles to doves
Swoop right over me every day
Sometimes I know what they're saying
Most of the time I don't

But I try to remember to say thank you anyway
Because a message is a blessing
Even when we don't understand it
The fireworks are still going off
Though it's not independence day
But even if it was
I think we're all feeling really awkward
About celebrating our independence
In this world where we are
So clearly not free
I write poems about reclaiming my body
And I make the men around me uncomfortable
What else is new?
It is summer and I am alive
The gold of finches, butterflies, and bumblebees
Season the sky like daytime fireflies
And hot air balloons float like great giant flowers
They make me smile every time I see them
The same way that dolphins do
Though there is still snow on distant mountains
We've been peppered with enough scorching heat
That I should relish the mornings
That are sometimes cool enough
To make me impatient with my old dog
When I forget a sweater
The nights are my favorite kind of warm and breezy
That help me find my gratitude
Scorch and relish
Scorch and relish
Like a wave
I guess it's a blow torch that has my attention after all
It is summer and I am alive

SWEET

You will have to choose this
At some point
If I am what you want
You will have to choose
To make thinking of me
An act of pleasure
And to be generous with your stories
That is how we move forward
In the choosing
To dwell
In the sweetness of each other
And in the choosing
To move through the pain
Some days
It will feel like running
Through honey
And that is when
You must remember
To stop
Bend down
And take a drink
Because it is sweet, my love
Oh how sweet it is

ALL I KNOW

I don't know

If it's you and me

I only know, that after all this time

When I think of what I want

When I, with breath half-held,

Let my heart weigh in

All I know

Is that I want you to come to me

Let me take you by the hand

And without words

Lead you to my bed

Where I will lie upon your chest

Still and silent

So after all this time

Our hearts may

Finally speak

SACRIFICED

I do not want to
Intrude on your
grief
With my joy
I am too light
For you
Right now
Airy and playful
Cotton candy
When you need meat
Something raw
And bloody
Something that has
Been sacrificed

MOTHER'S DAY

I don't go out on Mother's Day anymore
After all the times
The cashier or server or some other lovely person
Wished me
A happy mother's day

The first time it happened
I said, "oh I'm not a mother"
And in that moment
I gave the poor woman
All of my awkwardness
Which didn't seem like a very good thing to do
To a person who was just trying to be nice

The next time it happened
I said, "thank you"
And felt like a fraud
Taking credit for participating
In a gauntlet that I sat out, benched
Which didn't seem like a very good thing to do
Accepting credit I didn't earn

The third time
I said, "I'm just the mother of a dog"
A bitch, I guess? (True)
But I said it like I felt it
Like I was worthless
Which didn't seem like a very good thing to do
(To myself)
As if my dog isn't
The greatest creature in the universe (True)
And that it wasn't the best job in the universe
To get to hang out with him and care for him
And teach him while he cared for and taught me
(Is this how parents feel about their kids?)

So now, on Mother's Day
I stay in
I cry a little and call my mom
And make myself French toast
That I eat in front of the flowers I bought myself
Not for Mother's Day
But because I buy them every week
To remind me that I deserve them
And also to remind me that
It's okay to enjoy and care tenderly for
Beautiful things
That are not meant to last

CRACKED

If you see me
Naked in the woods
Crying
Mind your business
I have just gone crazy
But that is no concern of yours
Is it?
That I have gone crazy
Finally cracked
Under the pressure
Of living in a body
That I keep being told
Is not mine

SURRENDER

I surrender
Like the match
Surrenders
To the flame
By being
Consumed
Transformed
Dispersed
As heat
And light
I surrender

NOT LIKE US

I kissed him
But he wasn't you
His scent didn't make me want to hold my braid
To my face and inhale him
Like yours did
Reluctant to wash my hair, my clothes
My body
He is smart and kind
Cautious and sensible
A person who believes
They still have time
Not like us
Not like us
The polite smile
My heart offers when he calls
Is no match
For the quiet distant thunder
That rumbles through my soul
When I hear your voice
The disinfected truth he shared
Though perfectly profound
Does not ignite me
The way our naked mangled honesty
Sharp as the glare of the sun off a mirror
Blinded me and set me on fire
The adequateness of him
Steals my words
For the only way I can write about him
Is by comparing him to you

His sweetness
Is a cheap candy bar
Cloying and unsatisfying
While you taste like
The piece of dark chocolate
I eat each night
While I smoke a joint
The dessert I crave
So rich and strong
That it bites me back a little
And makes my heart ache
To feel so alive

MEANT

I hate that we don't speak
That we never named what was between us
That we never found the place
Between then and now
Where I can love you again
Without feeling
Like a damn fool
I hate that we let the words
We never said
Pile into a wall between us
Instead of using them
To build a boat
That could save us both
From the flood
Of my tears
I hate that I will never know
If your silence says
I meant nothing
Or that I meant
Everything

GLASS

I found glass
On the floor today
From something I broke
So long ago
I almost don't
Remember
How can it still
Be there?
The glass on the floor
(Waiting to cut me)
I've cleaned it so well
And it was so long ago
Maybe even yesterday

COST

I smelled the past
This morning
Faintly
As I sipped my tea
It was sweet
And a little smokey
Honey in mezcal
Pulling at my heart
Begging me to follow it
Down
The hot and dusty path
Of what could have been
Welcoming me out of the moment
Where my tea is warm
And my garden green
Promising me endings
I've already read
For the simple cost
Of right now
I did not go
I did not go

CONSTELLATION

I am a constellation
        I said to some of

The great loves of my life
As we lay
      a
        m
          i
            d
              s
                t
      The dirt and dog hair
On the kitchen floor
Near the moving carpet
              By the breathing plant
            A story of perfect chaos
        Mathematically precise
      And cosmically unknowable
I am old and being born
        Made of love
        And fire
I am a constellation
On the kitchen floor

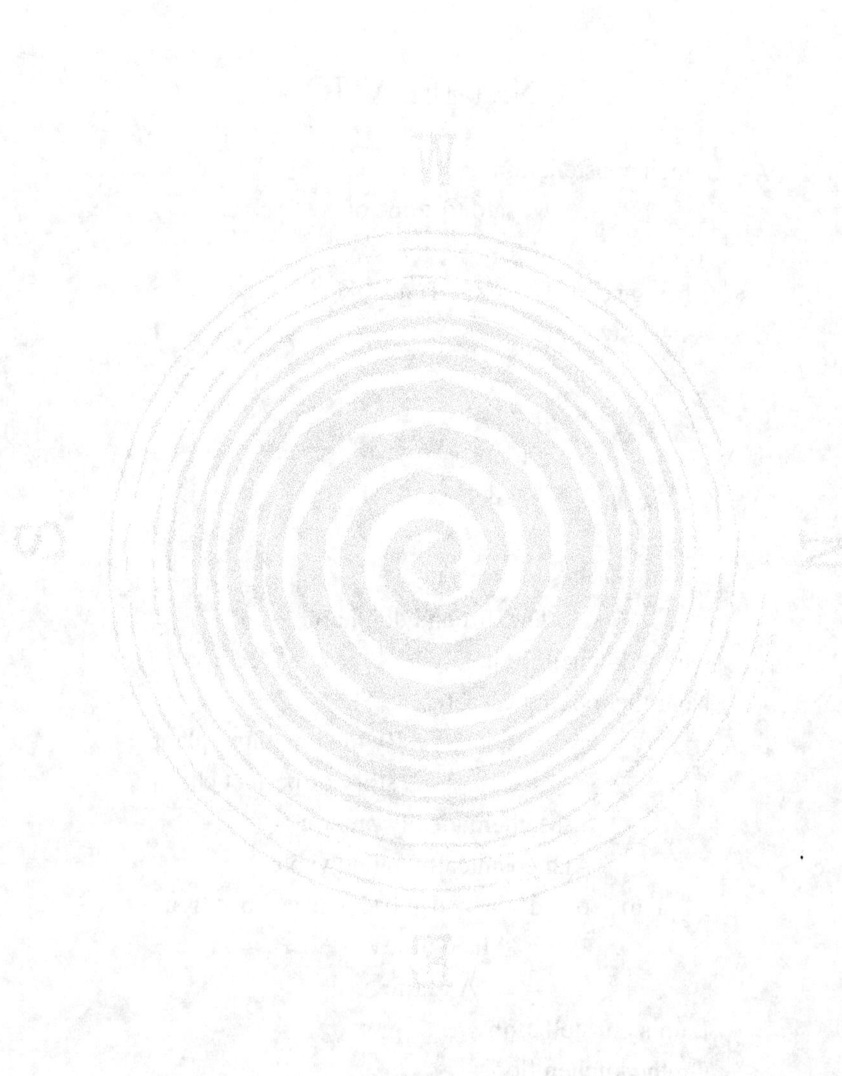

ATARAXIA

When I think of loving him
My arms, they open wide
And he would never clip my wings
To keep me by his side
I thought I'd never leave you
But I know I cannot stay
My spine is strong enough now
For me to fly away
I'll always love you madly
But I won't go to war
My life, it is my own now
I'm not angry anymore

THE GATE

When I went to look for my heart
Unsure it was still there
Or if it had wandered off (with you)
What I found was a gate
Heavy and iron and high
It looked ancient but I'm certain
It wasn't there before (you)
I tried to pry it open
But it would not budge
So instead I began
To tear down
The walls on either side
Each brick heavy
With another story I don't need
Carefully, I dislodged an
"Oh but they did this to me"
And discarded it next to a
"What will people think"
When I got to the brick of self-doubt
It was so dense with "shoulds"
I thought I might be crushed
Under the weight
But once that was down
The rest crumbled so easily
And my heart stood free again
Except for the iron gate
Which I left there
For the one with the key
Or the one wise enough
To just go around

INSTEAD

There is a
You and me
Somewhere
Together
Sitting at our kitchen table
Together
On Sunday mornings
Laughing
And grumbling at each other
And loving
There is a you and me
Somewhere
Together
And I don't know
If we should
Try to be them
Or just
Be happy for them
Instead

WORK

If you want it to be her
Work on seeing her
Work on hearing her
Work on knowing her
This is how you love her
And if you don't want
To do that work
Let her go
Because you don't want it
To be her

EVERY WORD

In the time
When you were not here
And I only knew you
In my heart
I would walk to the woods
Today in the snow
Surprised by how like the sand
It treated my footfall
Sounding like something
Both wrung and poured
Or maybe sifted
Sluice is a funny word-
And the sound my boots make
As I walk across the path
Into the woods
Mining gems
Sluice, crunch, sluice, crunch
All the way to the three sisters
Giant stones I each call grandmother
For their ancient beauty and wisdom
Which they share
When I let them hold me
Today, they whispered
"You speak the truth of your existence
With every word you say"
To which I replied
Just the same as the birds cry out
When they take flight
I am love
I am love
I am love

WHEN I REMEMBER

I don't know if we come out
On the other side of this thing
Holding hands
Or on opposite ends of the world
But I do know
(When I remember)
That I'm glad to be walking
This part of the path
With you

NORTH

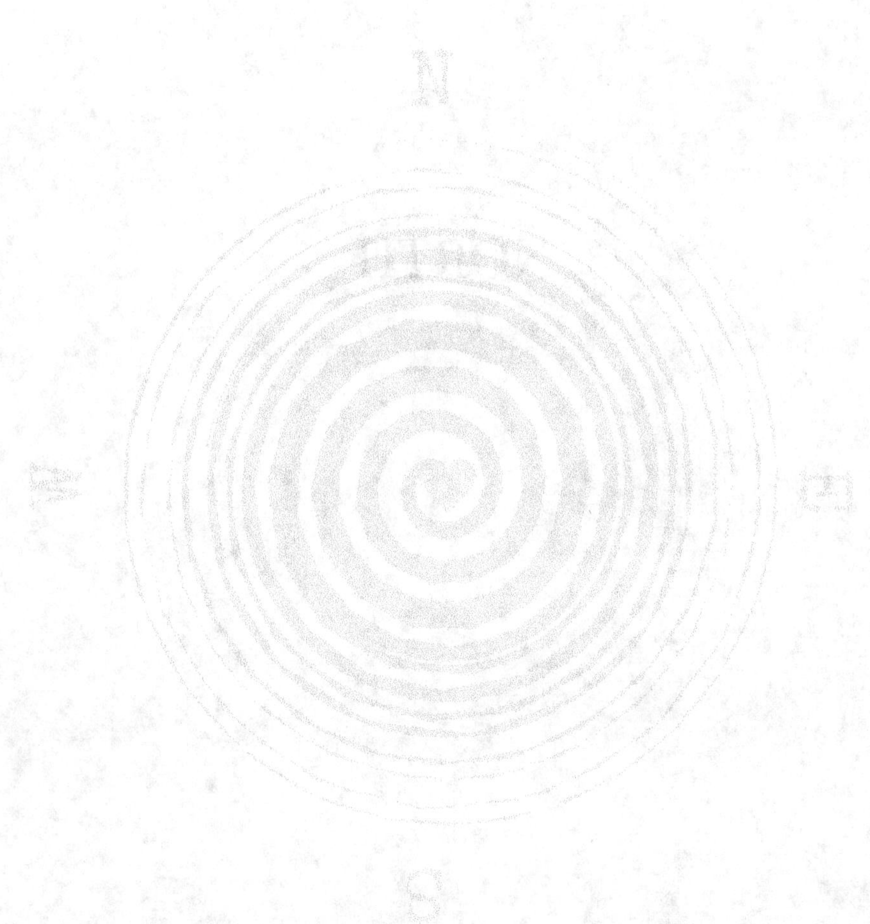

Make love
Make it for yourself
Make it to yourself
Until you are so full
That love overflows from you and
You cannot help but share it
And in doing so
Change the world
Make love
Go feel alive
For god's sake
Feel alive

CONSTANT

In this world
They say that
Change
Is the only constant
But I love you
And I will always love you
That
Is my only constant

IMPOSSIBLE THINGS

Impossible things happen all the time
How I could breathe before you were mine
And bumble bees fly and the moon glows
And spring breaks through the winter snows
Like every color in my eyes
And you between my supple thighs
Rain that falls on sunny days
The feminine and all her ways
Pine and poplar as one tree
The quantum leap of you and me
Galaxies are born and die
Elephants will sometimes cry
Impossible as bumble bees
This love we make will set us free

GATHER

None of us knows
How long we have left
So I gather the moments gently now
With purpose
The shape of this leaf
The smell of that flower
I listen carefully to the stream
And I wonder
If I will get to
Gather any more moments
With you

IF

If I let myself
I would miss your butt
It's gotdam perfect
I didn't even know that mattered
Until I saw your butt
In the hall light
And I could not help myself
But to bend over
And bite one sweet cheek
If I let myself
I would miss your lips
Hypnotizing as they were
For how I could not
Watch you speak without wanting
To slip my tongue
Between them
If I let myself
I would miss your voice
Part southern
Part courts
All of everywhere
I have ever been
And everywhere
I have ever wanted to go
If I let myself

DEAD BRANCHES

I stare at the patches of earth
Appearing
Around the melting snow
A flower, a heart
And a brontosaurus
I wonder what they know
How long the dead branches above
Will keep them from disappearing altogether
And I think of the people
I've loved
Who I see no more
And want to thank them
For letting me go
I don't know why
Those things are connected
But it seems true that they are
So I sit barefoot
In the sun
And try to let go of
The habit
Of wondering why
I am here

DISROBE

The blossom is
Awakened
By the heartbeat of the earth
She feels it move
Up her roots
Breathing life into her leaves
Tethered wings
Steering her toward the sun
So warm and loving
That she cannot help
But relax
Disrobe
And allow herself
To be seen

PERFECTION

I had to attract
A lot of broken people
To show me how broken
I was
To transcend
My brokenness
To release
My stories
To embrace
What was left
And (finally) see that
Nothing was ever broken
After all

N
W
E
S

R O O M

I went back to the woods today
I reclaimed them
And myself
My body
My right to be here
I watched the dragonflies
That come in so many more colors
Than you would imagine
(Did you know there is a black and teal one?)
It felt overgrown since I'd last been there
(Was it with you? I can't remember)
I sat on a constellation of ancient rocks
I call the grandmothers
One by one
And asked for help
"It is not yours to carry," said Mintaka
"You are safe," said Alnilam
"You are perfect," said Alnitok
The grandfathers didn't speak to me
They didn't know what to say
And just wanted to hold me
So I let them
I cried and my tears went by with the stream
I thought about what to say, what to do
(Were you with me?)
The swing we played on is gone
It only lasted as long as our love, I suppose
The rope is still there though
Someone tied a foothold
And it looks a little like a noose now

I didn't cross the stream
My eyes were too hazy with tears
And I thought if I fell in
I might fall apart completely
I never saw the mallards
But when I ducked behind a tree
To cry my tears out of view
I found the message you left me
Campfire stones arranged in a heart
And I cried a little more
I took off my shirt
Letting my soft belly hug my waistband
I almost took my bra off too
So powerful was my desire
To claim my body and
My space in this world
I kissed the trees
While the cottonwood floated down on me
Like great soft jellyfish
In the sea of blue sky
I stopped to watch it and the sun
Imagining I was on the ocean floor
And only had to swim toward the light
To break through the surface of the water
Into a world where everything is alright
A bicycle bell dinged
And the bikers whooshed by
But I held my ground
Arms spread wide
And took up my space

N
W
E
S

Just like I did on the way home
When the man jogged toward me
On the narrowed path
I did not shrink
I claimed my space
So he could see
That there was room
For both of us

N
W
E
S

BETWEEN

The bridge has burned between us, love
But do not be afraid
        See, in that fire I burned too
      It's how my wings were made
Our love, it wasn't born here
          It has no human name
We had to walk through fire
To remember why we came
       Please don't fear you've lost me
        A bridge don't mean a thing
For the heart moves not by walking
         But only with its wings
The past is not the way to go
          Not for you and I
Who needs a bridge between us
       When we both know how to fly

ENDING

I watched a movie
About the end of the world
And I thought about you
And me
And what the fuck else is there
If the world was really
Ending

GHOSTS

The secret that I've found
When I remember that it's there
Is to love a person freely
And the moments that we share
Memories only haunt me
When I'm chasing after ghosts
And forgetting who I am
By loving someone else the most
But when I don't remember
And I've fallen on my sword
May I not forget
I need only love me more

UNCONDITIONALLY

I want
To want
You to be happy
At least I think I do
I try to wish you well
But still
There is some small part of me
A little smiling devil
Who hopes
That your life
Will never be quite as sweet
Without me—
A low-fat, carob-chip existence
That's a little less rich
Than the full-flavored life
You could have had with me
Good and nice and fine
But never as satisfying
As the real thing
And so I don't know
If I will ever truly
Love you
Unconditionally
But I can
Unconditionally love
The me that tried

IT'S ME

I was listening
To the past today
It was coming through the speaker
As some song playing the story of me
When I loved you so much
I let it rip me apart
When I was hurting so bad
From longing and
The never-healed wounds
Of past lives
Bittersweet
Like chocolate without sugar
And an aching heart
It's me it's me it's me
And that's all it has to be

THE WEDDING

I married myself
On a walk today
We didn't plan it
It just sort of happened
There was a log
So I jumped over it
There were promises made
And tears of joy
The stream played a song
And the birds danced with me
It was cold but
I felt so much warmth
From being in love
And alone

NOSTALGIA

You played with my hair
We talked about porches
And the past
It was good
And it was sad
It was comfortable
And it was strange
Strange that it was comfortable
Sad that it was good
Time wouldn't let us
Stay there
Or anywhere else
Which is probably
Good and sad
Strange and comfortable

CRAZY

I used to think
I was crazy
For loving you
Broken as we both were
Broken as we are
But the only crazy thing
In this world
Is to believe
That we were ever broken
And the world was ever not

THESE BODIES

When I remember
How short time is
Here
In these bodies
(How can something unreal
Be anything but)
And I forget everything
I've lost
(I've lost it)
I wonder why I am not
Spending
Every moment I have
Watching your face
Touching your hand
Noticing
How these bodies change
Next to each other
So much of this life is folly
It is absurd
Not to be loving you
All ways
In these bodies

ANCESTORS

Is each snowflake
(I can't help but wonder)
An ancestor
Floating, swirling, dancing
Past my window
Cheering me on
Witnessing
The arrival
Of a promise fulfilled
Millions of tiny angels
Filling me with their hopes
Showing me that I am
Both one of kind
And one of many
Reminding me
That we are free

EITHER WAY

It's gonna be hard
                    Either way
Do you want
Hard alone
                Or hard together
There is no wrong answer
            There is only
            the choice
        Which is hard enough

LIKE GODS

I want you
To quit this world you think is real
And run away with me
To a little corner
Just for us
Where we will speak
Like gods
And fuck like
Animals
And live out the rest of our days
In love

NO RULES

Lover
We can do this
Softly
We don't need the world
To frame us
We can tiptoe
Into the garden
And you may climb a tree
While I lie in the grass
There are
No rules

POSSIBLE

What would be possible
If you believed you were god
Would you walk more gently
Upon this world you've created
Would you pause to admire
Your hawk soaring above
And your spider weaving a tapestry
Between two branches of
The magnificent lilac bush
That you wove
What would be possible
If you believed you were god
Could you finally love yourself
And worship yourself
So you could love your neighbor better
Could you mend and heal
All that has been broken
What would be possible
If you believed you were god
Maybe
Everything

ALL OF IT

We are not here forever
My loves
Not in this moment
(or anywhere else)
Eat the thing
Wear the thing
Say the thing
Make love to
All of it
And that will be
Enough

GREAT LOVE

When I am old
Older than now
I will gather the children of the children
Of my sisters
And when they say, Great Aunt Kiki,
Tell us about that time
I will say it was time of fear
Making a futile grab for power
While Love waited like a patient mother
For the people (children, really)
Who were so mired in fear
Masquerading as hate
So manipulated by a system of greed
That they had forgotten they were people
And so, also forgot
Others were people, too
They made a lot of noise for such a little bunch
Like a fly
Banging against a sunny window
But Love watched
Bright and quiet
A lighthouse in a storm
As the ships of fear
Found their way
Or crashed upon her shore
I don't remember the details
But I do remember
The Love

N
W
E
S

For times marked by great fear
Will always be marked by
Great Love
And that push and pull
Like the water against an oar
Is what moved us forward
Then I will gather them
These children of the children
Of my sisters
I will gather them
In my arms
And I will kiss them
Until they squirm
While my heart whispers
Thank you
Great Love

THE ANSWER

The answer
To the question
Is always the same
Get quiet
Hear your soul
Love

COMPASS

You think your path is forward
To the left or to the right
You spin your compass every day
And lie awake all night

But if you sat in stillness
You would know that it's not east
There's no peace in your heart there
In that place you felt the least

If you slowed your breathing
You would know that it's not south
The past is but a memory
Where the truth came out your mouth

If you could trust your instinct
You'd know that it's not west
The place you found to blossom
Isn't always where you rest

If you used only your logic
You might try to find your worth
By changing your direction
And moving farther north

But your path knows no direction
It's not linear, you see
It doesn't just move forward
By steps or by degree

Your path is like a spiral
That goes up and it goes down
Each footstep is supported
When you make your heart the ground

Your path is only made for you
There's nothing you should fear
That place you think you need to go
Has always been right here

So sit down in the shade, dear
And take off that heavy pack
Stop staring at your compass
You've never been off track

About the Author

Kerry Love is a writer, an artist, and a teacher. *Fine Tuning* is her second book of poetry and a follow up to *Not Fine*. Her first novel, *By Chance*, was written with her best friend, Jill. You can find her walking around Colorado looking at birds, touching trees, or wandering around the basement of the biology building searching for her classroom.

kerrygretchenlove.com
@kerrygretchenlove